Unveiling

Poems and Paintings

Unveiling

Poems and Paintings

Robert Hershon
Elizabeth Hershon

Hanging Loose Press,
Brooklyn, New York

Published by Hanging Loose Press, PO Box 150608, Brooklyn, NY 11215.

www.hangingloosepress.com

Printed in the United States of America 10 9 8 7 6 5 4 3 2 1

Hanging Loose thanks the Literature Program of the New York State Council on the Arts for a grant in support of the publication of this book.

Cover art by Elizabeth Hershon
Book design by Nanako Inoue
Authors' photo by Michaleen Hershon

ISBN 978-1-934909-74-4

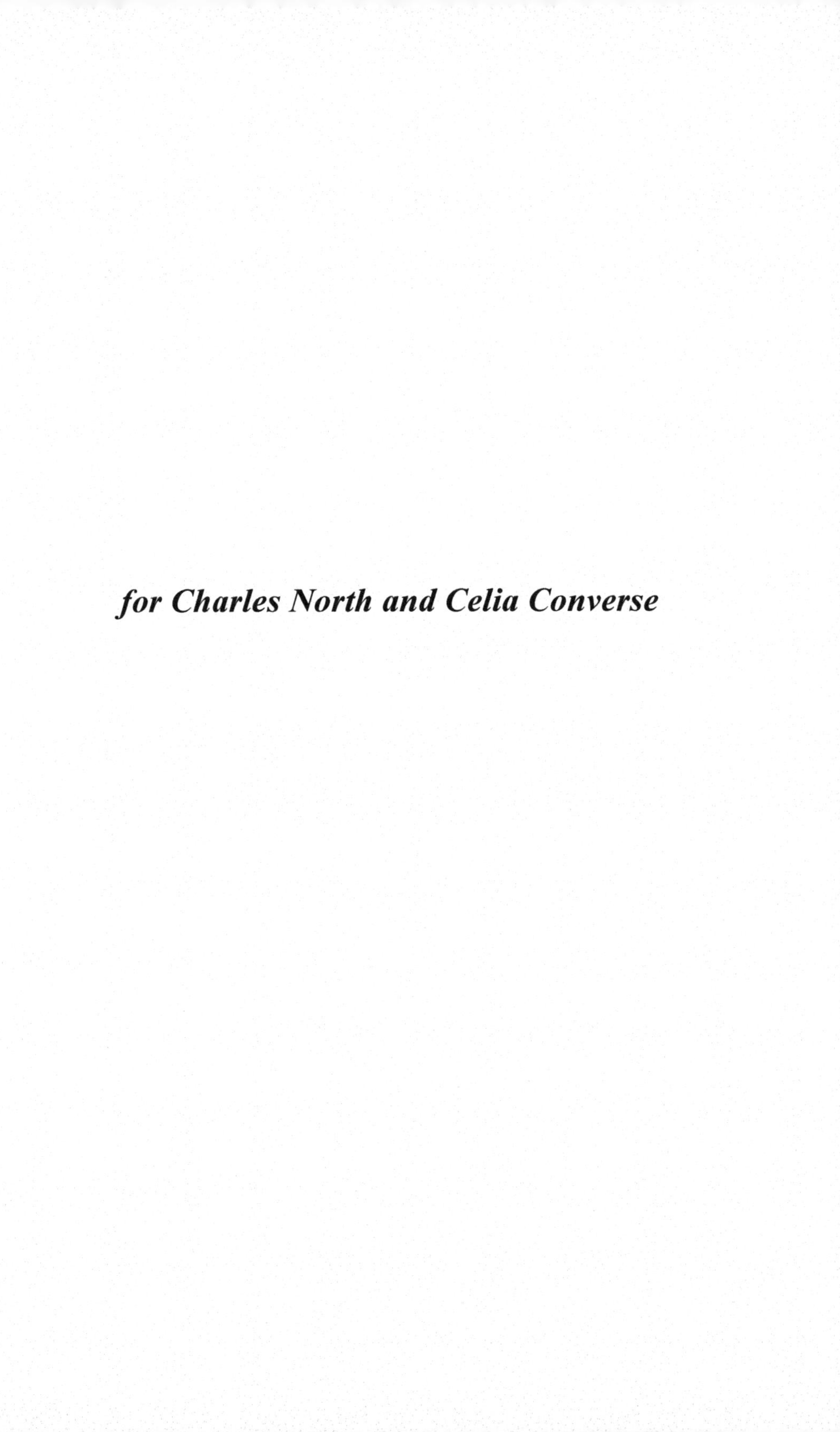

for Charles North and Celia Converse

Bob Hershon was one of four co-founders of Hanging Loose in 1966; he remained active with the press until his death in 2021. A widely published poet himself and a native Brooklynite, he was part of New York City's poetry scene for more than a half-century.

He also maintained a close connection with the New York art world, counting many painters among his friends. He brought his passion for the visual arts to Hanging Loose magazine—or perhaps he brought the magazine to the visual arts. Each issue presents a portfolio of paintings and cover art by one artist.

Elizabeth Hershon, Bob's daughter, is a painter, ceramicist, poet, teacher, and the art editor of Hanging Loose. She lives in the East Village, but grew up in Brooklyn. Bob approached her in 2020 with the idea of doing a book together: her paintings and his poems. The result is *Unveiling*.

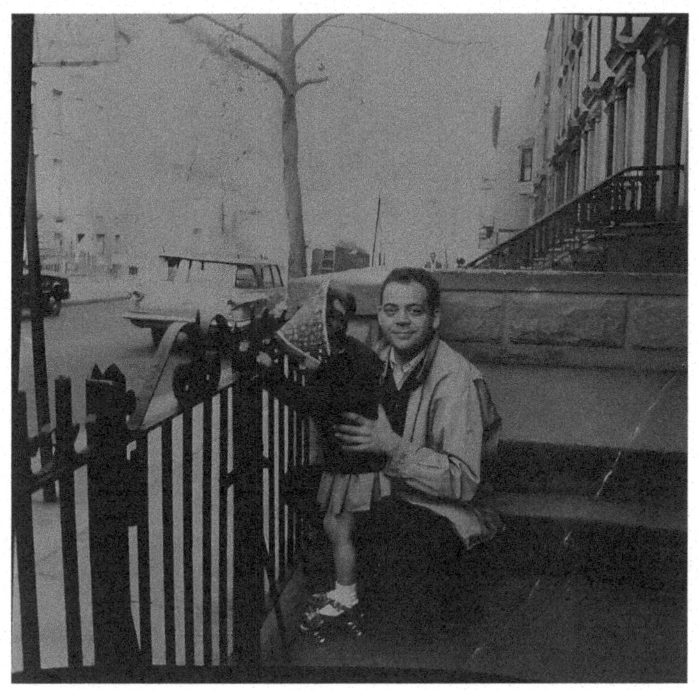

Dear Dad,

Thank you for asking me to do this book with you. You have always validated my desire to be creative, and through your eyes I could see my own worth and talent as an artist. Our work does not have that much in common but our bond is our mutual respect for each other's work. Your encouragement has always been important to me and is even more so now, with your idea of this collaboration. I admire your lifelong journey as a poet. I am sorry that you will not get to see these final results, but I cherish the thought that you wanted to do this with me. It is an honor to be here with you in this book.

Love,

Lizzie

CONTENTS

Restless In Spring

Do not aspire to be a carefree mayfly
The mayfly lives just one day

And it might not be a good day
despite the sincere wishes
of the other mayflies
It might be black of sky with
pounding rain and birds
of relentless hunger

So you might consider moving on
and becoming a june bug
buried in the mud and secure
with your seventy loving eggs
until light penetrates the dark
and shrivels you up

What now? There are no
July bugs—You might
just try staying human

Photographer

She stops to take
a photo
of the ocean
in Palm Beach
It's much like
the ocean
in New York
but it's the ocean
of record
and she must have it
jellyfish admire
her sense of responsibility
and would applaud
if they could
I will join them
(endless clapping)

Chatter

I did the Saturday puzzle on Sunday and
the Sunday puzzle on Saturday and I
watched a thousand hours of cops and robbers
when my friend assigned me the task of writing
a baseball poem, since right now there is no
baseball except in memory so I thought of
the Miracle Mets and then the Boys of Summer
but they both seemed frayed from overuse and I
began to think of the teams of my boyhood, call them
the Boys of Early Spring—Eddie Stanky and Pete Reiser
and Cookie Lavagetto, Kirby Higbe and Ed Head and that perfect
baseball name, Dixie Walker, brother to Harry the Hat Walker,
and remembered more as a bigot who wouldn't play with
    Jackie Robinson
than as an outfielder, but I didn't know that when I was
ten and we had the only television set at 946 Bushwick Avenue
and I watched the games by myself with a bag of candy corn
the cheapest loose candy Woolworth's sold, assuming
the Dodgers and I would grow old together (twelve,
    fourteen, beyond)
and wondering why all baseball announcers had Southern accents
and now the rich players and the even richer owners have finally
decided to play some baseball and I guess I'll slump down and
stare at the games, by myself again, but without candy corn

Potty Mouth

I would like to meet
the man who coined
"potty mouth" and
plunge his head into
a bucket of shit
for, say, an hour or so
just to make the point that
there are no fucking dirty words

All Right

Everything's all right   I'm wearing my water buffalo coat
it's 92 degrees, I'm in Water Buffalo, New York,
No that's not right, I'm in Hot Water USA, but everything's all right
Was it DiMaggio hit three doubles for the Cincinnati Reds, not bad for
a dead guy. No, that's not right. He's a dentist, a Seventh day Adventist
a mentalist, he was sent to head the rescue effort but he got picked off.
The Arno is not always gentle.
The high water mark is at eye level. Paintings rush
downstream.   I can tie my shoes with my eyes
closed, with one hand, in the dark, standing on my head.
The nurses are running fevers and the doctors are running away
We're burying canned body parts in the garden. It's almost
first light, we'll be all right

Key Ring

Why do I still carry these heavy keys?

This one was for the Print Center on Varick Street, which I left eleven years ago. No one in that building would know me now.

This was for the '97 Toyota I sold to Omar for $400 three years ago. It ran for twenty years and It was my friend, but true friends don't insist on getting parked.

This one opens the door at the top of the stoop. It hasn't been opened in fifteen years. One day movers will carry out all I own, maybe including me.

And what is this key for? I don't remember it but I'd better keep it. It might be the key that unlocks the universe or the doorway to oblivion. I might be engaged with that door.

Still Life

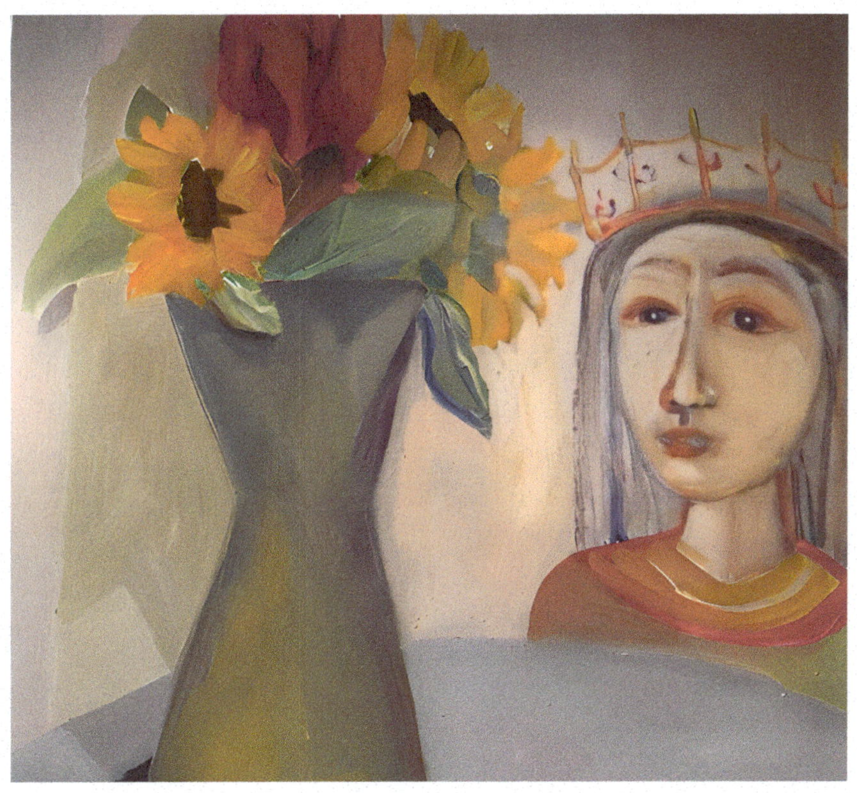

Lullaby

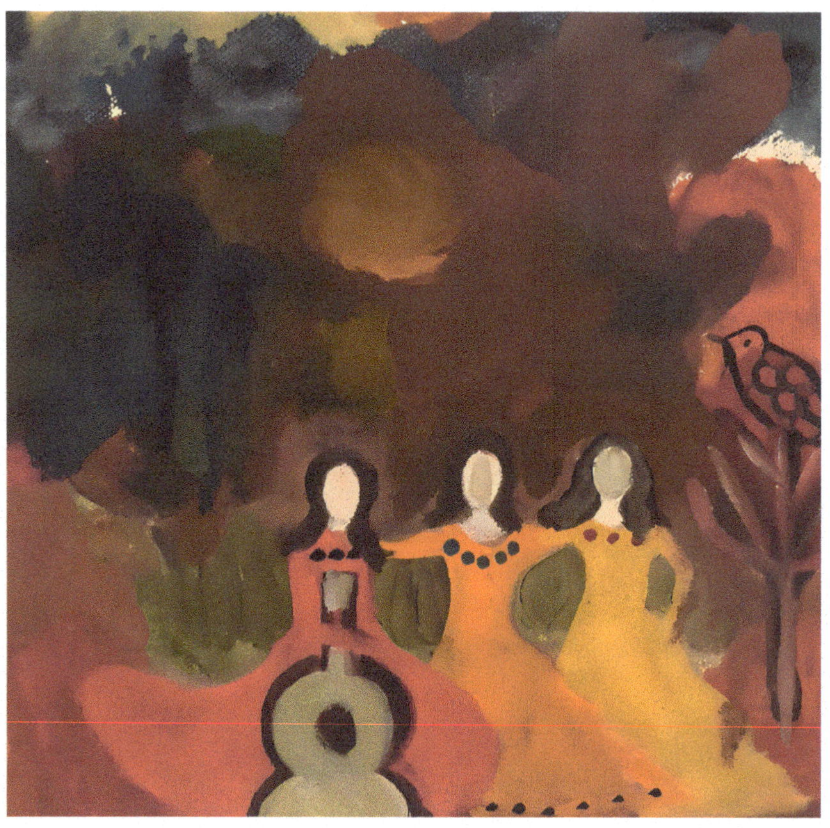

After the Wedding

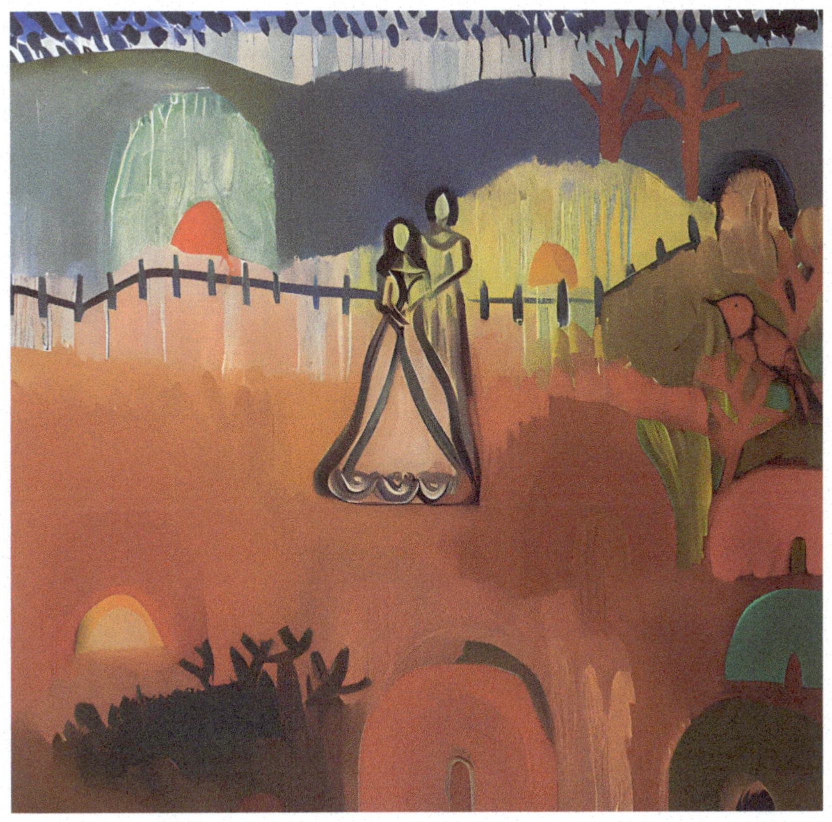

Cliff Town

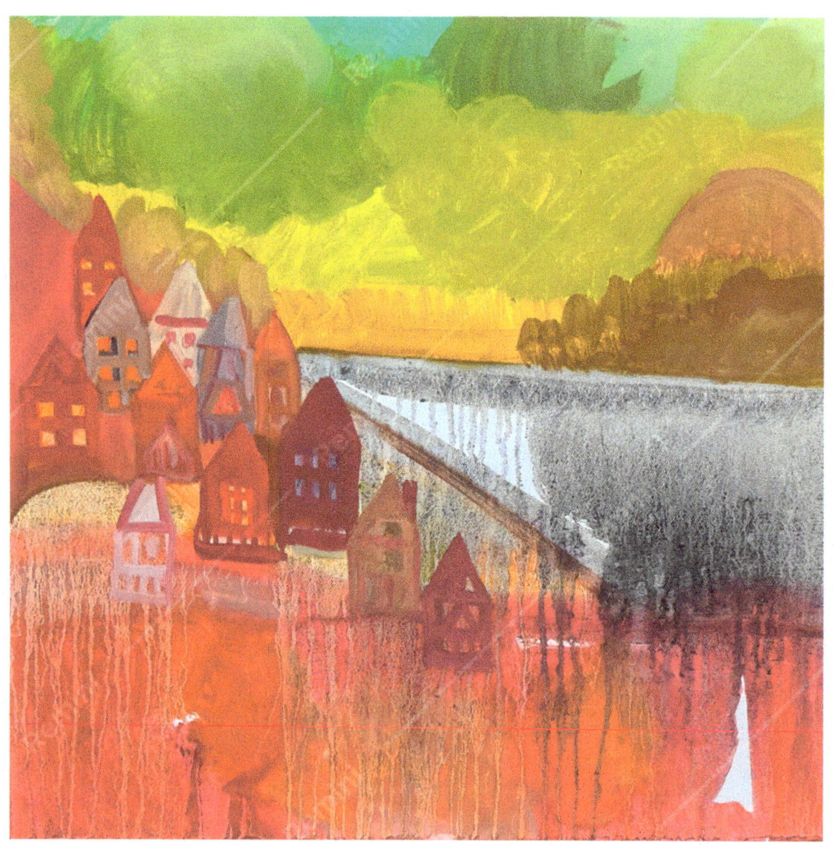

Last Night in Malaga

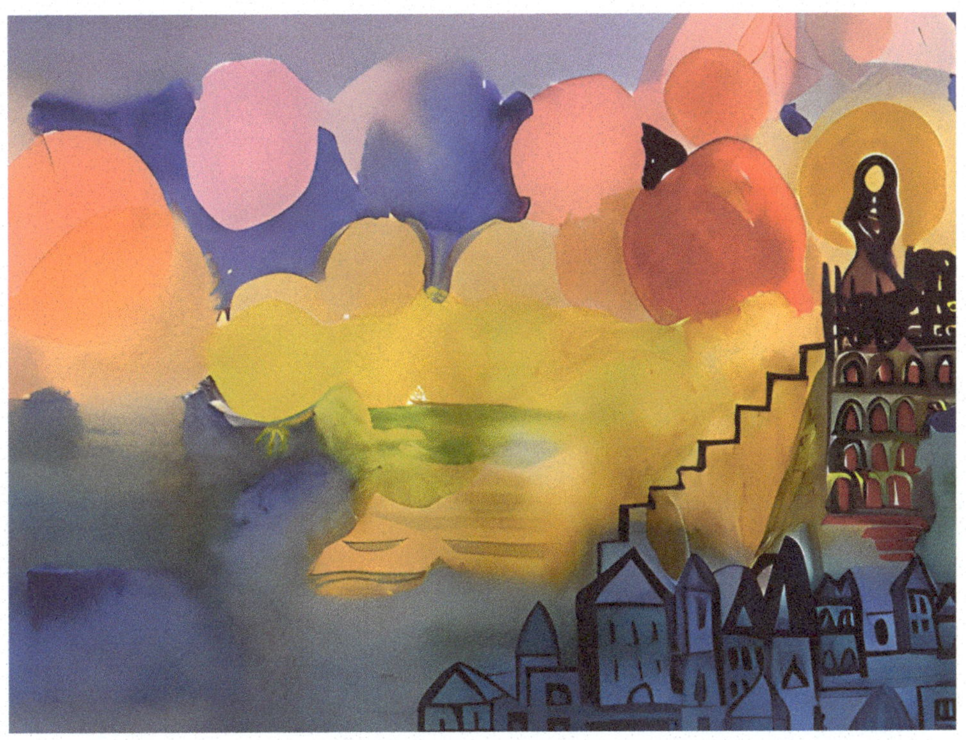

Blue Fruit

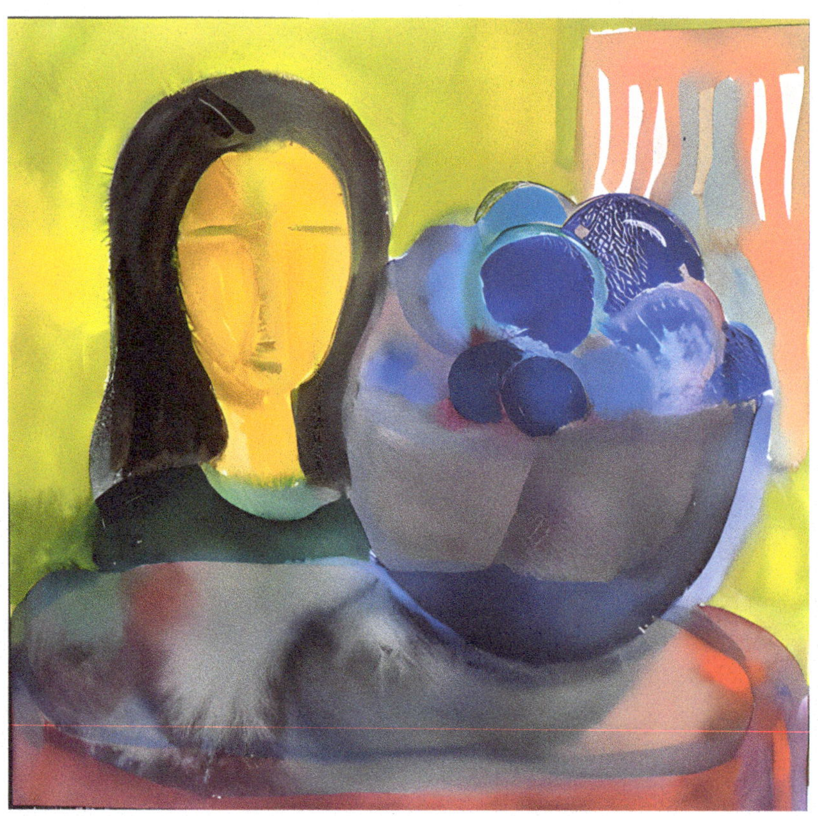

An Old Cowhand Went Riding Out One Dark and Windy Day

I have managed to empty my head
almost completely, creating vast hollows with
crusty thick walls, except for that one dim room
reserved for old song lyrics
which permits neither additions nor erasures
so today just when I think I have achieved total
mindlessness I find myself humming
Ghost Riders in the Sky, and Rudolph the Red-Nosed
Reindeer. No, not humming. I know the lyrics, every
relentless word, and when I try to segue into, say,
Bartok piano solos or Etruscan poetry (for instance)
a thundering herd of red-eyed cows insists on center stage
"As the cowboys rode on by him
he heard one call his name" (Hey, schmuck, we always said)
and the cruel reindeer won't let Rudolph play their games
so the room is filled with sweating bodies until
there is no room to breathe, just flesh on flesh
sweat and stench, and an ominous red glow
through the fog and it's too late to switch to
Some Enchanted Evening

And So the Poor Dog Got None

To fall asleep. Write new verses to Old Mother Hubbard. Write a letter to Liz Swados. Take a Klonopin. Name actor siblings: 4 Marx Brothers, 3 Lane sisters, 3 Barrymores, Curly, Shemp and Moe. Write a letter to Harvey Shapiro. To Ed Woods, to Jayne Cortez, to Tom Eagan, to Ron Schreiber, to Paul Violi. Take another Klonopin. Write new verses to Friggin in the Riggin. 2 Crosbys, 2 Fondas, 3 Carradines. Stop. She went into town to buy him some shoes but when she got back he was reading the news. How are you I am fine how are you I am fine. Write an acceptance speech. Write a rejection letter. Write this poem. Or not.

An Infusion

First they have to take some of my blood
so they can be sure it is a match
for the blood they are about to give me
It goes round and round
In the waiting room of the infusion center
I try to decide who's there for blood and
who's there for chemo. My ashen contemporaries
have canes and walkers but there is also a
boy in a Red Sox cap and a very pregnant young woman
No one makes eye contact, but the nurses know some people by name
In my infusion room I have my own television and time to watch
two and a half Special Victim Units. I'll never know if the professor
is really a serial rapist but I can live with that suspense
My arms are covered with elastic bandages. The nurses can
never find my veins

My Blood

My father, who was afraid of my mother's craziness, of her screaming and paranoia, told my sister and me that we had to deal with her, that she was our responsibility because we were *blood* relations and he wasn't. He had merely been married to her for fifty-five years, just passing through. But he was my blood relative and I carry the inheritance in a dented bucket.

As the technician prepared to take blood from my arm—four tubes this time—I said that I envisioned, in a dark sub-basement of the hospital, a huge iron vat of my blood, trembling a bit as though something was trying to break through to the surface. I could tell she was wondering when to call for help.

I've never been scared by the sight of my own blood, swirling in the dentist's spit bowl or soaking through a Band-Aid, but I was stunned the first time I stood up after surgery and blood came pouring from the foot-long opening in my abdomen. The bad-tempered physician's assistant jumped back. You almost got my dress, she whined. But then: glub. She was drowned—and the blood flowed through the halls, down the stairs, into the cafeteria. Blood sandwiches were served. Hollowed out and neatly folded, I floated back onto the island of hospital corners, waiting for someone else's blood to replenish me.

Thursday

Thursday, July 27

Morning

waiting for coffee
smoking reading
a 1961 ladies home
journal

bugs on the big
window
some inside
some outside

wanting

Afternoon

sitting on the queen
red tens on his thigh
the weather will clear
by noon

look for kings
his mother said

rain ending by two
the three of clubs
torn the five the nine
the jack in the toilet

weak sunlight
around four

Evening

the same black bird
flies toward the house
again

we do not sense
the variety of his circle

shadow not shade
the grass rapidly ungreen
the ice melting
another dinner

probably the same
black bird
probably the same
last boat on the bay
probably the same
fallen channel marker

we fight during dinner
i slam a door you throw
a plate the children hide
we attack our guests

still it grows dark
again

Night
a moth in the room
wings against the window

thunder, the storm moving
closer, children will wake.
you dream always
of lightning.

the moth will fly
into my mouth. i will
eat its dusty wings.

lightning. the same face
at every window, a dead gull
on the lawn. headless.
a thousand silver fish devoured.

torn moths on the waves.
scream of a boatman. vomiting
hunchbacks under the house.

darkness again. insane whispers
of children in night. then silence.
fraud. everyone awake. waiting.
wings.

Report to the Blue Guard

the problem: to remember
the dreams of the day

and i will forget
tonight again
and lie in the sun pits
uninterrogated
painted many colors

far below the bridge
standing on the bridge
with the blue guard
smoking
swaying

By the Sea

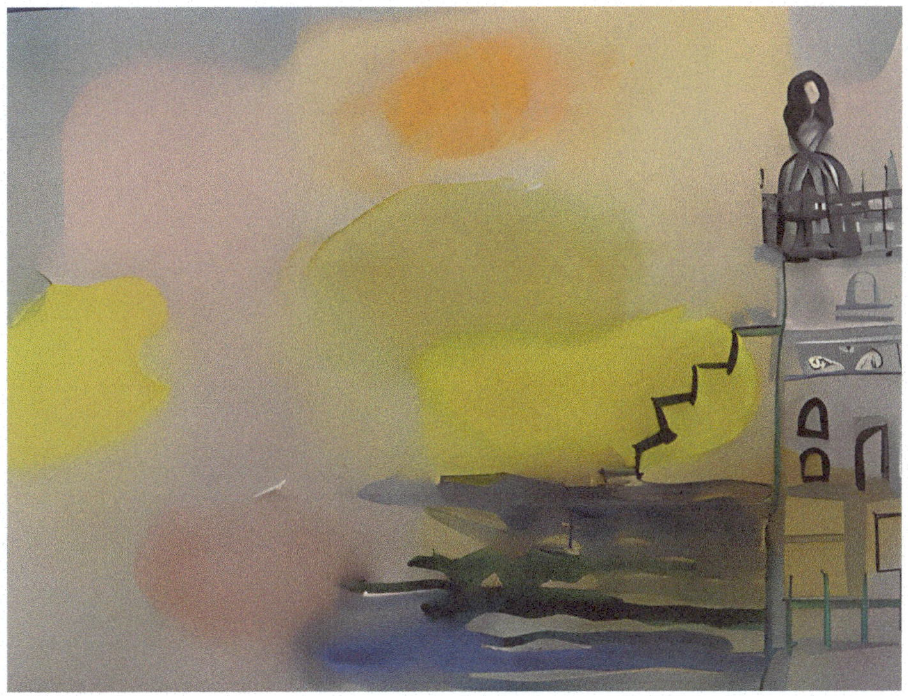

Wedding

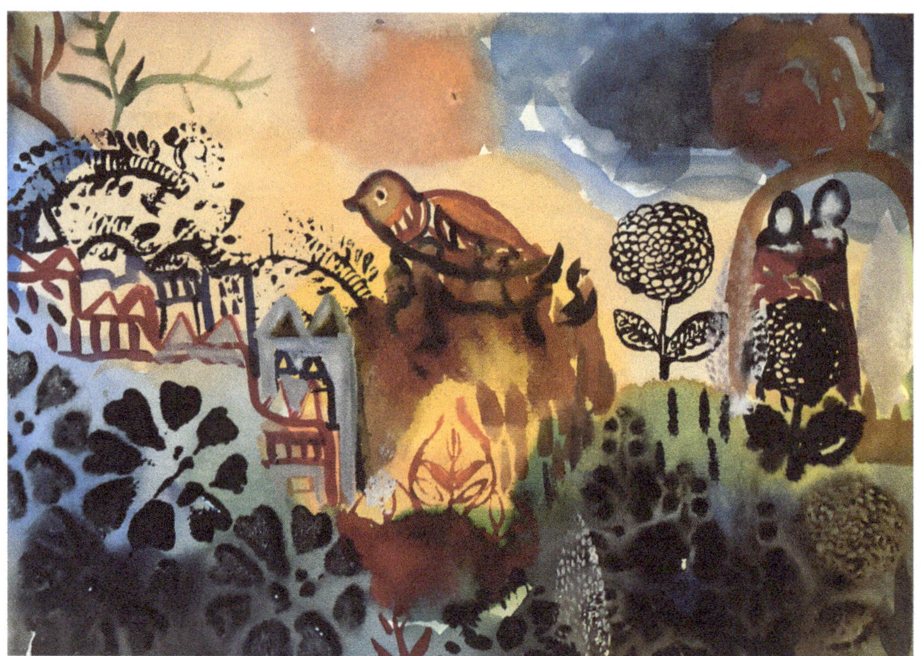

My Mother's Owl

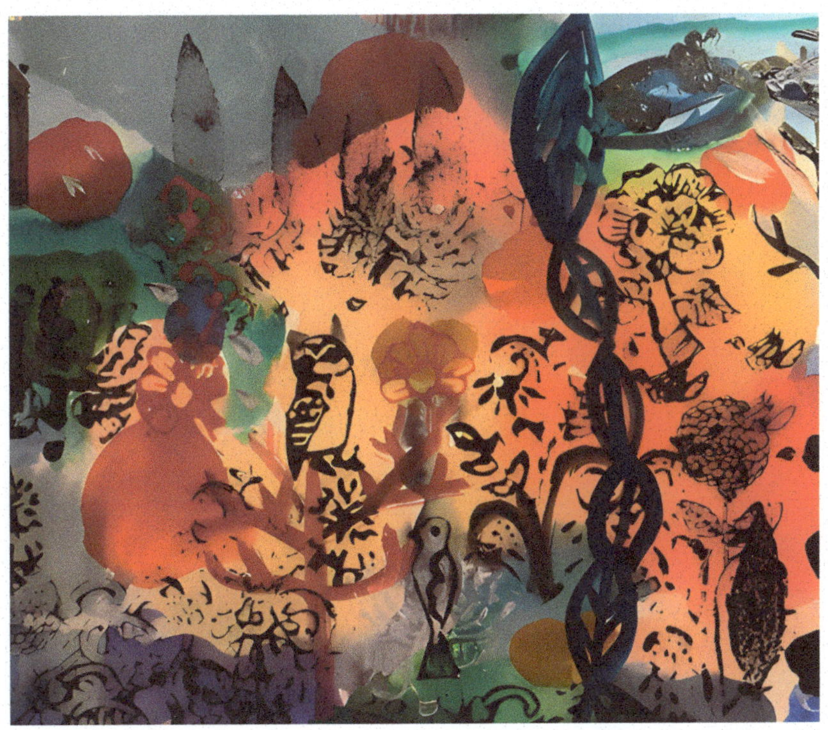

Pretty Polly

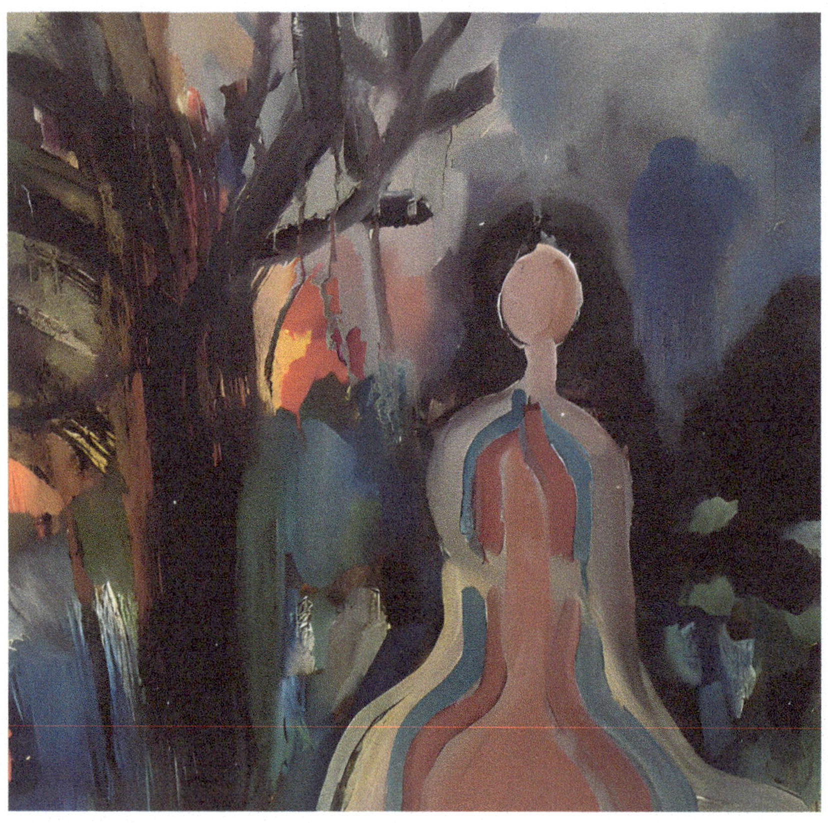

Reunion

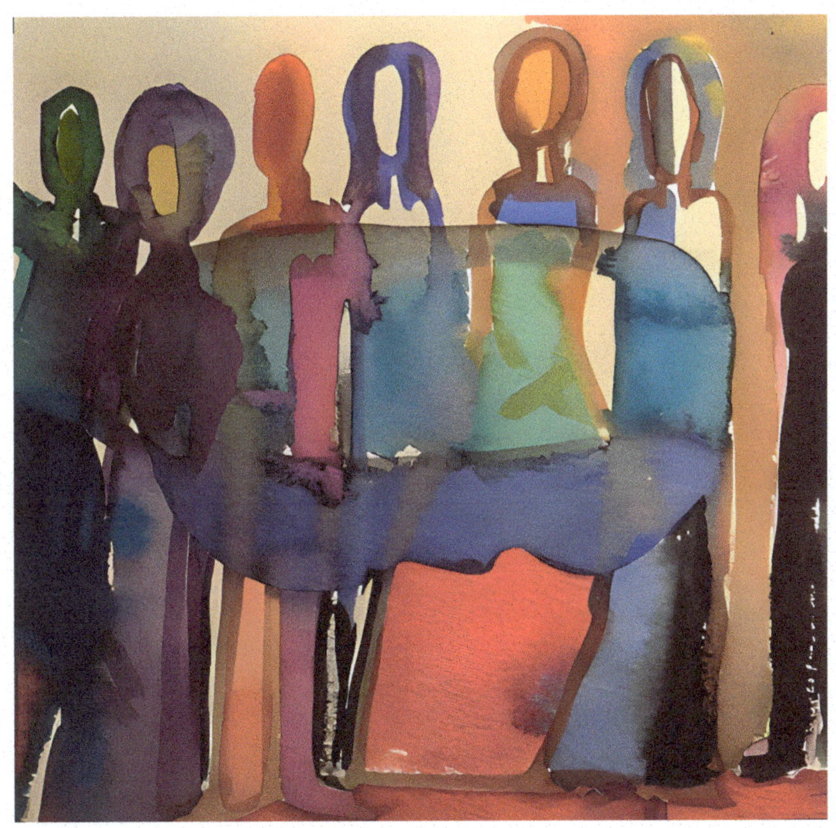

The Visit

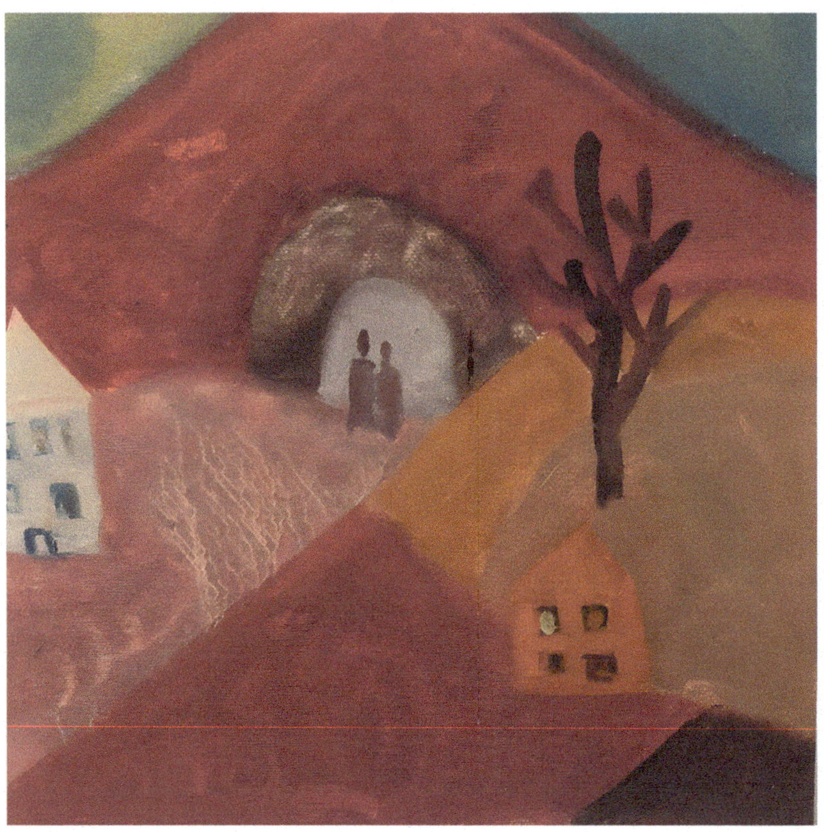

Visit to a Brooklyn Zoo

hello charlie?   this is jack
in san diego   look
i've got a cancerous rhino
maybe a month left in him
can you use him?
and a three-legged ocelot
you could prop her up
can you use her?

the children run ahead
let's go see the goddamn monkeys
let's go see the shitty bears

hello charlie?   warren in st. louis
what's the story on the stork?
oh yeah?   too bad   look
i've got a concave camel
and an elephant we had to cut
his ears off
can you use them?

the children run ahead
there are wild dogs
in the silent birdhouse

and a zebra   it's got no face
how about a paralyzed hippo?
you could float it
can you use them?

the children run ahead
past the stiffening mandrills
they're hungry
even hungrier than before

listen charlie
about the buffalo
the sores won't show
if you keep its back to the wall

Frank's Bar XII Adler Place
XII Adler Place Frank's Bar

Because of the shape of the hill
Frank's Bar is directly upstairs from XII Adler Place.
Yet Frank's Bar and XII Adler Place each have a separate entrance at street level.
A back staircase connects the two. You can walk right into Frank's Bar and stay in Frank's Bar or you can walk right into XII Adler Place and stay in XII Adler Place.
Some, however, prefer to walk into Frank's Bar, go downstairs and drink in XII Adler Place.
Others prefer to walk into XII Adler Place, go upstairs and drink in Frank's Bar.
Still others like to have a drink in XII Adler Place, go upstairs and have a drink in Frank's Bar, then go downstairs again and have another drink in XII Adler Place.
But they're really different sorts of bars, so people who drink in XII Adler Place usually stay in XII Adler place and people who drink in Frank's Bar usually stay in Frank's Bar.
The owner of Frank's Bar is Frank. The owner of XII Adler Place is also Frank. But Frank doesn't run XII Adler Place. Frank Jr. runs XII Adler Place. Frank's wife helps him run Frank's Bar but never goes downstairs to see her son Frank Jr. at XII Adler Place. She watches television with earphones. Frank plays bar dice and dances the Tarantella when a customer plays G9.
Frank's bar and XII Adler Place share a common men's room. It's downstairs. It has two urinals. You might see a Frank's Bar drinker pissing at one and a XII Adler Place drinker pissing at the other. They would probably not talk. They would probably not know each other.
Now this was a while back. Everything has changed. Frank is very old. Bessie too. Frank Jr. had other plans.
So Frank sold XII Adler Place to Specs Simmons who used to be a regular at Frank's Bar. Then all the Frank's Bar regulars moved downstairs to drink with Specs at XII Adler Place and they became XII Adler Place regulars. No one drinks at Frank's Bar anymore. And no one knows where the old XII Adler Place regulars drink now.

All this happened some time after I left San Francisco when I
was twenty-five years old. I don't know a lot of the stuff
I used to know. You could write to Specs Simmons at XII
Adler Place to find out what's new but I don't know if you'd get
an answer. Unless you were one of the old regulars at
Frank's Bar. Maybe not even then.

Grocery Lists

I

i see myself in everything
charlies glasses red cars your eyes
myself in oval disapproval

walking through myself
in doorways holding the door
for the man just behind

a great foot for puddles
the disconnected face
muddled by the giant shoe

the red car the black car
the black car the dented door
the fluid shoulder hunching

they all look like me
until they move
there goes another

i see something just behind me
from the corner of my eye
just moving just lost

the red car the black car
the red car the black car
the red car the black car

II

i was blind blue apples
cabs all black death
of smoke lipstick

feeling my fathers face
with fingers immensely sensitive
his face like my face

and if i heard all poems
through your voice
all poems what then

arrested for feeling up statues
licking paintings
braille apollinaire

Swans Loving Bears Burning the Melting Deer

And he said, "The subject for this evening's discussion is poetry
On the subject of love between swans." —Kenneth Koch

great bears on fire
leaping from their caves
to watch the loving swans,

and the deer melting
at the lake's receded edge

the swans hate their necks
and would be green pigeons
sucking on sidewalks

i hate your sharp red beak says a swan
but you must kiss me

the burning bears are watching,
the sweet rabbits behind the leaves
shaking

the deer looks to the cave
sees nothing
melts

The Editors Editing

Nomi our neighbor
Asks Donna what are those
Guys doing out back
Sitting around the table
Table full of papers
And one guy goes blah blah blah blah
And the others all shake their heads
And go ahum ahum ahum

Then the oak leaves fall
Then the white garden furniture
Covered with gray city snow
Bluejay walks across the table
And down somebody's leg
Blah blah blah blah

There Are People Who I know Are Dead

There are people who I know are dead
and people I suppose are dead
and people who I fear are dead
and dead people long forgotten
and dead people who never leave

Dead people in the closet
wearing my shoes
Dead people on the kitchen floor
sprinkled with breadcrumbs
Dead people in my favorite chair
watching reruns of reruns
New arrivals pull up in cabs
Their shapes are blurred at the edges
but their beautiful voices remain clear

Hello, old friends, have a beer
Have a cigarette, what the hell now

The white horse standing still at
the end of the beach near Big Sur
at dawn, sixty years ago
That horse roams
through the house all night
a red eye, a flash of mane
That horse will never die
but it lacks the gift of conversation

Home

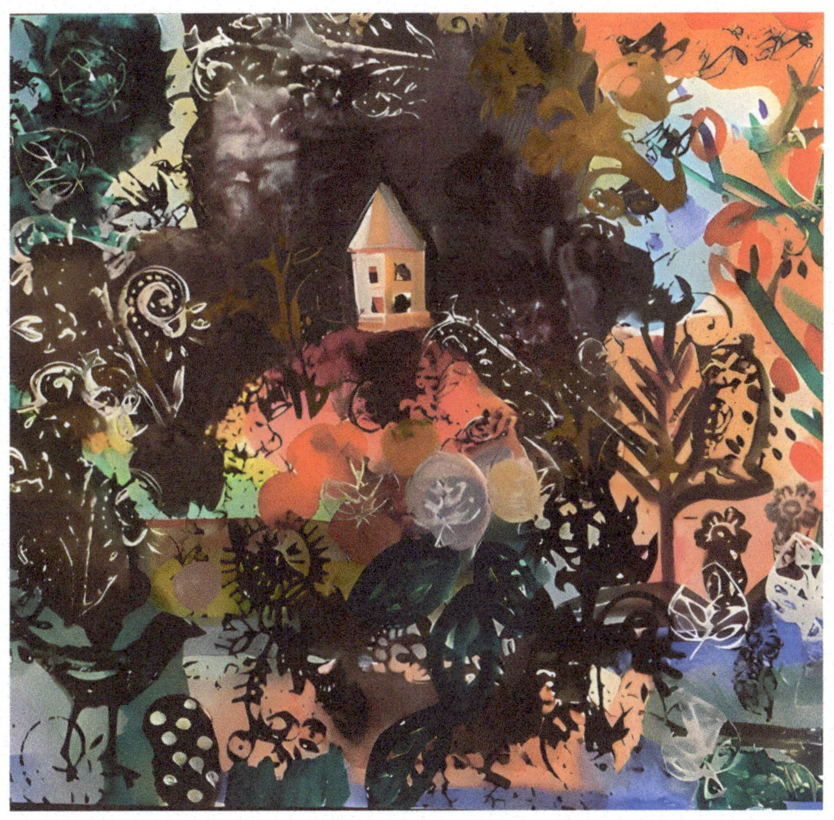

Gathering

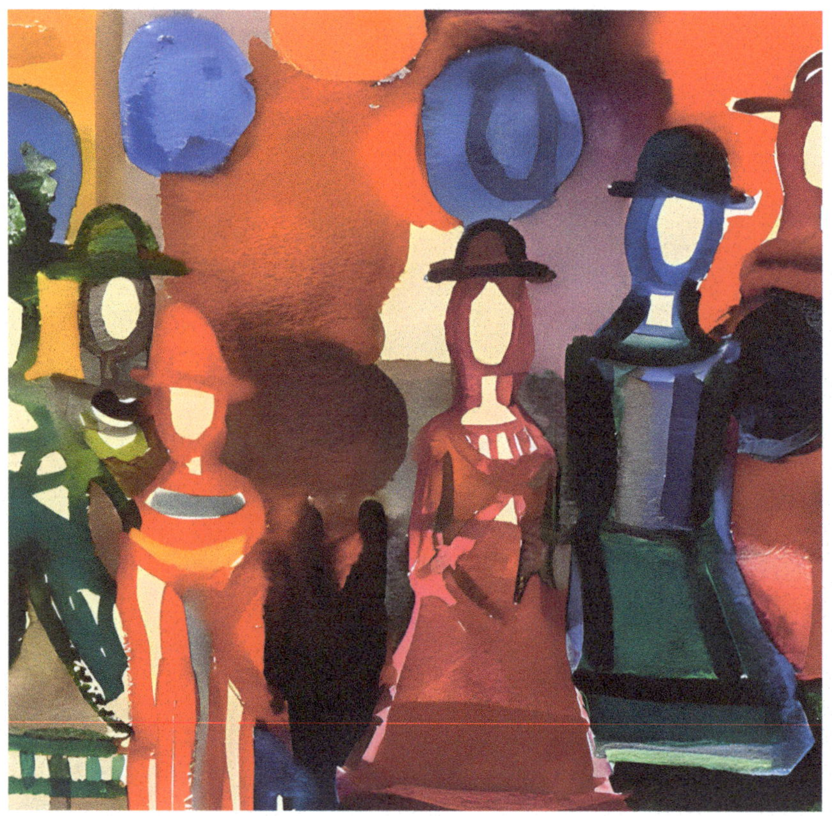

In the Clearing

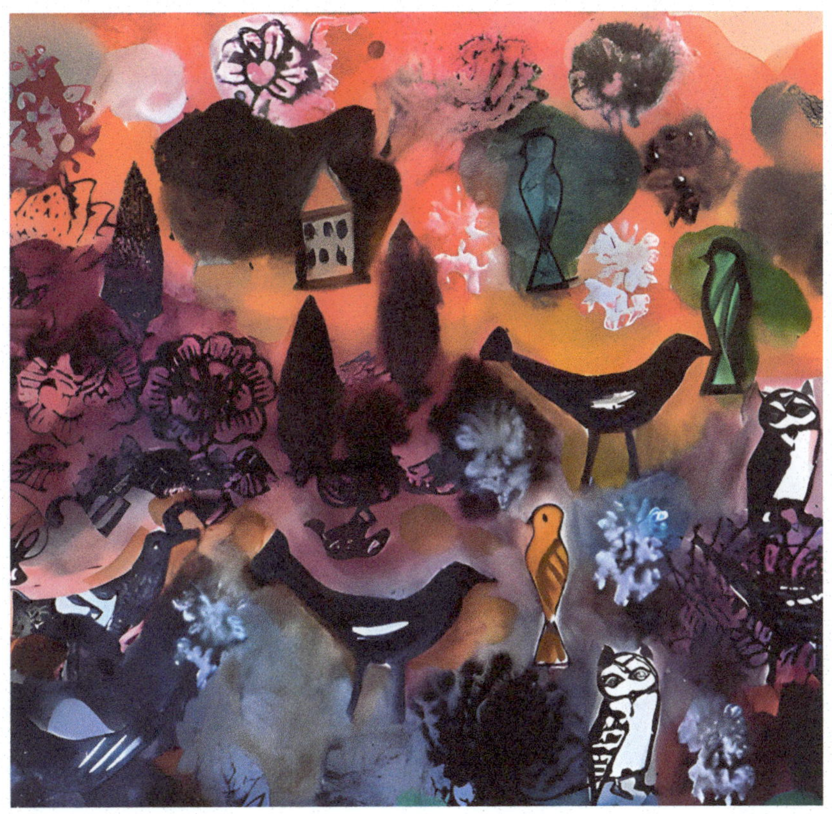

House in the Woods

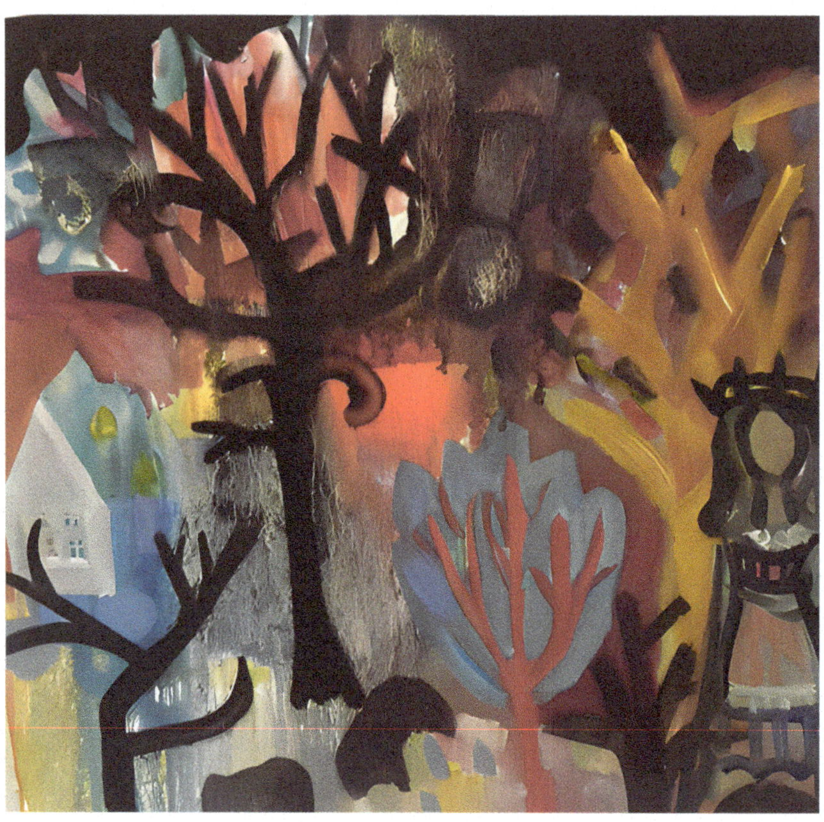

Ghost of You

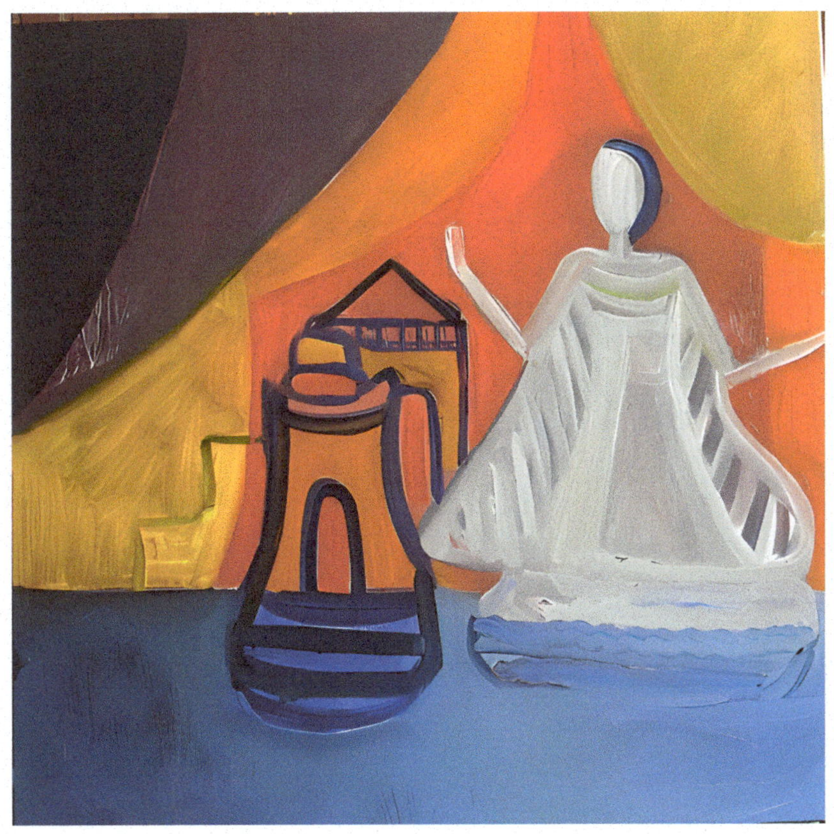

The Women

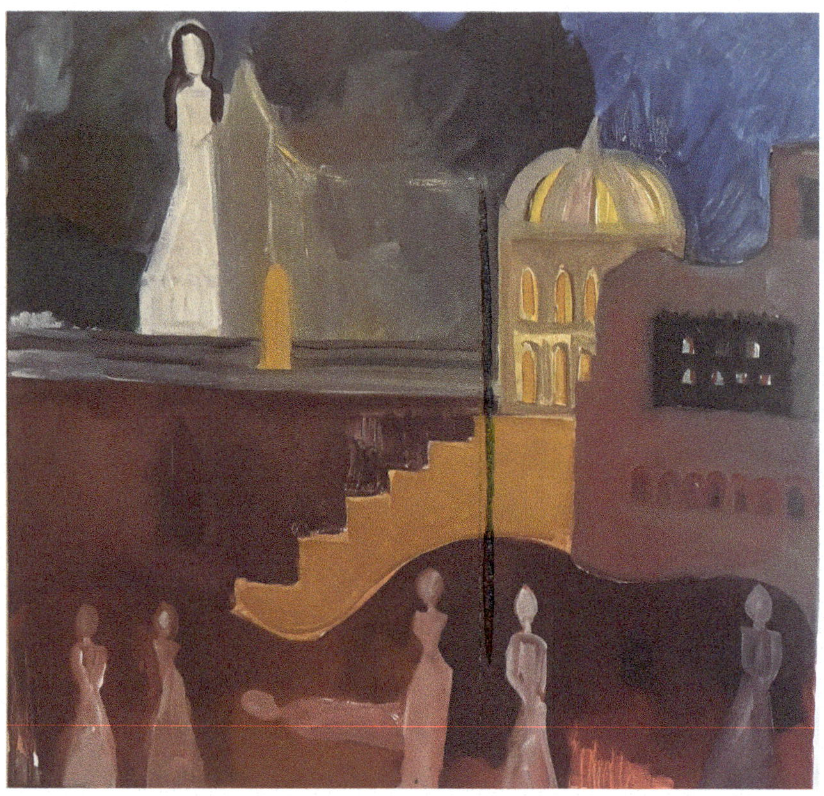

Unveiling

It's simple
Everyone in my father's family
dies of cancer
Everyone in my mother's family
dies of heart disease

It took a while for me to realize
that his family
and her family
added up to my family

Now I hear them arguing
in their adjacent graves
You take care of it
No, you

Note to Lizzie

After an arduous day yesterday, I went to bed very early but was awakened about 2 am by a dream in which Ron Padgett and I were disarming a murderer. I grabbed the guy and Ron grabbed his pistol. After this great adventure, I couldn't fall back to sleep and after a while I realized I was writing a poem in my head. The lines kept coming and I was afraid I'd forget them, so I got up at 4 am and went to my desk. Sometimes the poems that come to you in the middle of the night look like gibberish the next day, but I think this one holds up. And I think the manuscript for our book is now complete. I'll print out a copy of it, in sequence, for you.

The Camp

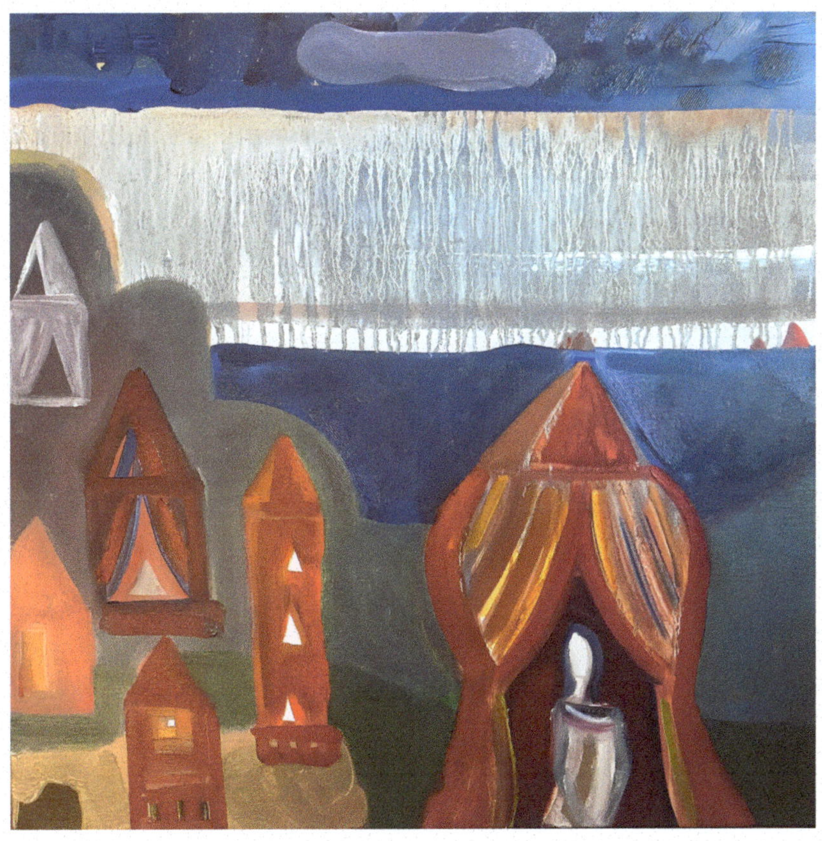